British Museum Object in

C000262945

The Colossal Statue of Ramesses II
Anna Garnett

The British Museum

© 2015 The Trustees of
the British Museum

First published in 2015 by
The British Museum Press
A division of the British Museum
Company Ltd
38 Russell Square
London WC1B 3QQ

britishmuseum.org/publishing

A catalogue record for
this book is available
from the British Library

ISBN 978-0-7141-5109-0

Designed by Bobby Birchall,
Bobby and Co.

Printed and bound in China by
Toppan Leefung Printing Ltd

The papers used in this book
are recyclable products and
the manufacturing processes
are expected to conform to the
environmental regulations of
the country of origin.

Note on dates
All dates follow I. Shaw and
P. Nicholson, *The British Museum
Dictionary of Ancient Egypt*,
London, 2008.

Contents

1 Ramesses II: the 'Younger Memnon'

[The Younger Memnon] struck me as simply the sublimest sight which in this sight-seeing world I had seen ... an emanation from some mystery of endless dawn.

THOMAS DE QUINCEY (*The System of the Heavens*, 1846)

1 The 'Younger Memnon'. This colossal representation of the ancient Egyptian pharaoh Ramesses II originally formed the upper section of a seated statue erected at the Ramesseum, Thebes. Granite and granodiorite. Egyptian, c. 1279–1213 BC. Height 266.8 cm.

In the early nineteenth century, the arrival in London of the upper section of a colossal granite statue representing the pharaoh Ramesses II (1279–1213 BC) challenged the conventional view of European art connoisseurs that ancient art was born in Athens and Rome. Egyptian sculpture was finally seen as being equivalent to the beauty of Classical sculpture in the round and Egyptian objects, no longer simply considered as artistic dead ends, were finally able to take their rightful place in museum displays from which they had previously been omitted. At the same time, Egyptology was becoming acknowledged as a legitimate field of study and the path was being laid for future generations of Egyptologists to tread.

Dubbed the 'Younger Memnon' by nineteenth-century travellers, the statue of Ramesses II is one of the largest examples of Egyptian sculpture in the British Museum. It measures just over 2.5 metres from the top of the headdress to the base of the ribs and just over 2 metres across the shoulders, and weighs around 7¼ tons. Even incomplete, the statue dominates the Egyptian sculpture gallery of the British Museum, looming high over the other objects in that great space. In its completed state, the whole colossal statue would have weighed around 20 tons and stood around 7 metres high.

Our modern understanding of the statue should reflect the perspectives of the ancient sculptors, those men who fashioned stone statues in the form of pharaohs, gods and the high elite for more than three thousand years. Such statues were much more than *objets d'art*; rather, they were cult statues, physical vehicles for the 'life force' of the soul, known as the *ka*, to which offerings were presented and rituals performed. While the pharaohs commissioned thousands of cult statues throughout Egyptian history, the reign of Ramesses II is notable for the construction of more temples, monuments and statues than any other reign in Egyptian history, creating a monumental legacy that eclipsed all others.

The visitor's first impression is of the immense size and characterful human features of the statue, but to the informed viewer its significance lies much deeper. As one of the first pieces of colossal Egyptian sculpture to be brought into the United Kingdom, its presence at the British Museum influenced a generation of visitors. For many, it was the first example of large-scale Egyptian sculpture they had ever seen. This book places the statue in the context of its ancient setting, its extraordinary modern rediscovery and its crucial place in the history of the Egyptian sculpture collection at the British Museum.

'Ramesses the Great'

The New Kingdom (1550–1069 BC) was a period of great prosperity and might in Egypt, although it was not without its ups and downs. The religious and political turmoil resulting from the reign of the 'heretic' pharaoh Akhenaten (1352–1336 BC) at the end of the 18th Dynasty was followed by the arrival of a new royal dynasty from a military family. During the 19th and 20th Dynasties (1295–1069 BC), eleven pharaohs would hold the name 'Ramesses', leading modern Egyptologists to dub the era the 'Ramesside Period'. The third pharaoh of the 19th Dynasty was Usermaatra-Setepenra: an individual better known today as Ramesses II, or Ramesses the Great, who succeeded to the throne of his father, Sety I (1294–1279 BC), in his teens and ruled Egypt for almost sixty-seven years.

The early years of Ramesses' long reign saw the initiation of a monumental building programme throughout Egypt. It was the most extensive in all of ancient Egyptian history, and included temples, cities and palaces. Notably, a new capital city and royal residence were established near the site of modern Qantir in the Eastern Delta: this harbour town was known as Piramesse, which means 'House of Ramesses'. This would remain Egypt's capital for the rest of the Ramesside Period.

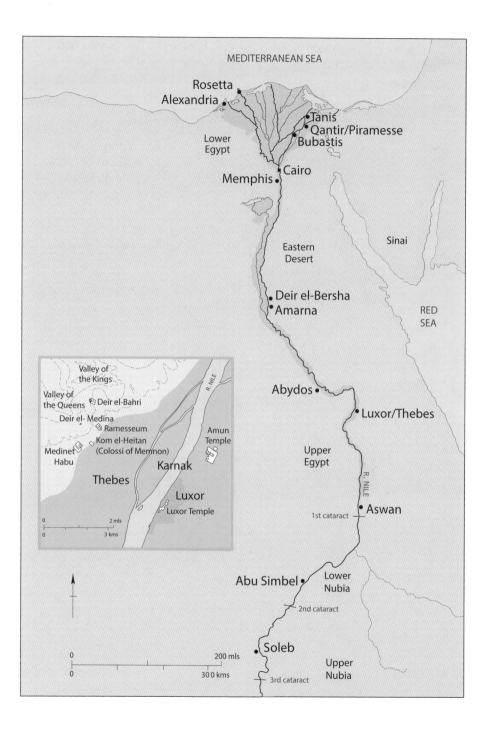

MEDITERRANEAN SEA

Rosetta
Alexandria

Tanis
Qantir/Piramesse
Bubastis

Lower
Egypt

Cairo
Memphis

Eastern
Desert

Sinai

Deir el-Bersha
Amarna

RED
SEA

Abydos

Luxor/Thebes

Upper
Egypt

1st cataract Aswan

Abu Simbel   Lower
Nubia

2nd cataract

Soleb

Upper
Nubia

3rd cataract

0   200 mls
0   300 kms

Valley of
the Kings
Valley of
the Queens   Deir el-Bahri
Deir el- Medina
Ramesseum
Kom el-Heitan
Medinet   (Colossi of Memnon)
Habu
Karnak
Thebes
Luxor
Luxor Temple
Amun
Temple

R. NILE

0   2 mls
0   3 kms

R. NILE

7

Ramesses defined the borders of a vast empire, established by his father Sety I, while extending his building programme outside of Egypt, most visibly south along the Nile into Nubia. The construction of vast temples proclaimed pharaoh's rule over Nubia, now partly lost under the waters of Lake Nasser.

Ramesses' military campaigns redefined international relations with Egypt's powerful northern neighbours, the Hittites (from ancient Anatolia), with whom he signed the oldest surviving international peace treaty after the Battle of Qadesh. Ramesses described and illustrated this conflict in great detail on his temple walls. The peace treaty guaranteed the subjugation of the Hittite empire and confirmed – in Egyptian accounts, at least – the strength of Ramesses II's kingship.

The most famous of Ramesses' Great Royal Wives was Nefertari, known for her beautifully decorated tomb in the Valley of the Queens, located on the West Bank of the Nile across from Thebes (modern Luxor); this was where the wives of the pharaohs were buried. Ramesses is known to have had many wives and to have fathered over eighty children. He himself was buried in a now badly flood-damaged tomb in the Valley of the Kings (KV 7), which originally contained sumptuous burial equipment but, like almost all of the royal tombs, was robbed in antiquity. The king's mummy was moved to safety during the Third Intermediate Period (1069–747 BC) and re-buried in a cache at Deir el-Bahri, only to be rediscovered in AD 1881 alongside his father Sety I and thirty-four other royal mummies. Ramesses' mummy now lies in the Egyptian Museum in Cairo, which means that we are still able to look upon the pharaoh who inspired the statue.

Memorial temples

During the New Kingdom, royal memorial temples were built to house the cult of the deceased (and therefore divine) pharaoh. They were also known as 'mansions of millions of years', a term which distinguishes them from the cult temples of the gods and emphasizes their permanence. New Kingdom pharaohs chose to construct their temples on the edge of the floodplain on the West Bank at Thebes, to serve as visual counterparts to their tombs, which were cut into the rock and hidden deep within the Valley of the Kings. The act of deliberately separating the memorial temple from the royal tomb may also reflect the desire for greater security from the widespread tomb-robbing of earlier monuments, including the royal pyramids.

The most common word for temple was *ḥwt nṯr* (pronounced by Egyptologists as 'hoot netjer'), meaning 'mansion'. It describes the primary function of temples as homes for the gods or as a focal point for the eternal worship of the pharaoh after death. Daily ceremonies were carried out in the royal memorial temples in order to provide for the *ka* of the deceased pharaoh, in theory for all eternity.

The cult statue was the central element of ancient Egyptian temples, and functioned as the physical vehicle for the manifestation of the deity: cult statues were protected and enshrined within the sanctuary, the doors of the shrine forming the interface between the divine and human worlds. During festivals, cult statues were brought from their sanctuaries and carried in procession within the protection of a sacred model barque or boat. The 'Beautiful Festival of the Valley' was the most important Theban festival during the New Kingdom. It marked the yearly visit of the enshrined image of Amun from his temple at Karnak to the memorial temples on the West Bank. Cult statues were only one part of the statuary programme of each temple, however: the Theban temple of Amenhotep III (1390–1352 BC) originally contained hundreds of statues representing the pharaoh and many deities, especially the lioness goddess Sekhmet.

Memorial temples were also an important part of the economic structure of ancient Egypt and incorporated extensive storage facilities for the enormous quantities of produce collected as taxes throughout Egypt. Each memorial temple had an individual name: Ramesses' was named 'The Temple of Millions of Years of Usermaatra, United with Thebes in the Estates of Amun, West of Thebes'; it is better known today as the Ramesseum.

3 A photograph of
the second courtyard
of the Ramesseum,
entitled 'Thebes
Rameses et colomns
Osiris', taken by the
Zangaki Brothers
in the late nineteenth
century.

The Ramesseum

Like his New Kingdom royal predecessors, including his
father Sety I, Ramesses deliberately situated his memorial
temple in front of the Theban Mountains, facing the Nile
and the temples of Karnak and Luxor on the East Bank.
The monumental architecture of ancient Egyptian temples
was intended to evoke the moment of creation when a
mound of earth was thought to have risen out of the waters
of chaos. Through the daily worship of the cult image, the
moment of creation was continually repeated.

The ground-plan of the Ramesseum comprises two
courtyards fronted by pylons (towered gateways), which
led to a hypostyle (pillared) hall and to an inner sanctuary.
The floor level gradually rises towards the sanctuary to
mimic the mound of creation, and the columns in the
hypostyle hall, in the form of papyrus plants, are intended to
represent the papyrus thickets dividing the mound from the

4 Upper section of
a colossal toppled
red granite statue of
Ramesses II, called
'Ra-of-the-Rulers', in
the first courtyard of
the Ramesseum.

5 (overleaf)
Aerial view of the West
Bank at Luxor (Thebes)
with the Ramesseum
in the foreground.

primeval waters. The memorial temple of Sety I at Thebes represented a peak in design, and its layout was copied in the plans of later memorial temples, including that of Ramesses III (1184–1153 BC) at Medinet Habu.

In the first courtyard of the Ramesseum stood a gigantic red granite statue of Ramesses II. This colossus now lies toppled and broken on the ground, but would originally have stood almost 16 metres high and weighed about a thousand tons. An inscription on the shoulder names this colossus as 'Ra-of-the-Rulers', explicitly associating Ramesses with the sun god Ra.

Smaller in scale but still colossal, the British Museum's statue of Ramesses originally formed the southern statue of a pair of colossal seated figures flanking the entrance to the western colonnade and the hypostyle hall of the Ramesseum, facing east. The head of the northern statue of the pair is still at the Ramesseum. The base of the southern

6 (above left) Re-erected lower section of the statue at the entrance to the western colonnade and hypostyle hall at the Ramesseum.

7 (above right) Rear view of the re-erected lower section of the statue at the Ramesseum, showing the inscription on the back pillar.

8 (opposite) Digital reconstruction of EA 19 upon the re-erected lower section of the statue at the Ramesseum.

statue – the lower section of EA 19 – was re-erected and restored to its original placement in the Ramesseum in 1997 by a French team led by the Egyptologist Christian Leblanc. A digital reconstruction has also been made of the upper and lower sections, illustrating just how striking the statue would have looked when complete.[1]

The statue

The fine quality of the colossal statue of Ramesses is illustrated by the details in its execution: cut from a single block of two-tone granite and granodiorite, the statue represents Ramesses in an idealised, youthful form. He wears the striped *nemes* headcloth surmounted with a now-fragmentary crown adorned with a frieze of cobras, or uraei, topped with solar discs. The stripes on the headcloth were only indicated in blue and yellow paint, which is now much faded. The remains of the royal uraeus, the rearing cobra intended to protect the pharaoh by spitting fire and poison, are evident in the centre of the

9 (opposite)
Detail of the face,
showing the
smoothness of the
skin in contrast to the
crown, eyebrows and
false beard, which
were deliberately
roughened.

10 (below) Detail of
the frieze of cobras on
the crown.

forehead. A ceremonial beard, a common feature of Egyptian royal regalia, is attached under his chin with the straps framing his face.

The face remains intact and displays a high level of workmanship; the cheeks are full and rounded, and the raised eyebrows frame the eyelids. The cosmetic-banded eyes gaze downwards: a conscious decision of the sculptor to make the colossal statue appear to be looking down on his subjects, the mere mortals below. This effect is still present today at the British Museum. The aquiline nose is intact and the mouth is well-defined with a sharp outline and two drilled cavities marking the corners of the mouth. The torso is more simplified in design and the pharaoh, bare-chested, wears a decorative broad collar around his neck.

Judging from the base of the statue that remains at the Ramesseum, when complete the seated figure wore a pleated royal kilt, called a *shendyt*, with a belt. The belt-buckle is inscribed with hieroglyphs in a special oval,

11 Detail of the broad collar and chest of the statue.

called a cartouche, that highlights a king's throne name or his birth name. They read: (cartouche) 'Usermaatra-Setepenra, beloved of Amun'. Usermaatra-Setepenra is the king's throne name, which means: 'The-justice-of-Ra (as manifested in the king) -is-powerful, chosen one of Ra'. The arms were held against the body and the hands placed flat on the knees.

The legs of the lower part of the statue are clearly defined, if schematic, with sharp lines indicating the tendons, and the feet have been lost. A badly deteriorated figure against the left leg represented a queen described as 'The [great] royal wife [....]'.

Both sides of the throne preserve scenes symbolizing the unification of Egypt, topped with the king's cartouches. They show the intertwining of the plants of Upper and Lower Egypt, the lotus and the papyrus respectively, by the Nile gods, and express the king's rule over a united country. These scenes, and the inscription on the base, preserve traces of yellow pigment.

Inscriptions

The act of inscribing a name onto a royal statue gave the image an individual identity, and perpetuated the name of the king after death. The Ramesses statue was originally supported by a back pillar inscribed with vertical registers of hieroglyphs cut sharply in sunken relief with interior details.

Two low outer columns, present only on the bottom half of the statue, contain the cartouche of Ramesses II upon the hieroglyph for gold, surmounted by the solar disc and feathers. The back pillar preserves an inscription in sunken relief, which runs all the way up to the king's crown. When both fragments are joined, it can be read in its entirety.

The right-hand column contains the names and titles of the king:

The Horus, Victorious [Bull] beloved of Ma'at, King of Upper and Lower Egypt, great of monuments in Thebes, lord [of crowns], Usermaatra-Setepenra, Son of Ra, Ramesses-Meryamun, beloved of Amun-Ra, king of the gods; he is endowed with life!

The left-hand column preserves part of a speech by Amun-Ra:

Words spoken b[y] Amun-Ra, king of the gods: 'O my son, of my flesh, my beloved, lord of strength, [Ramesses]-Meryamun! I have given you millions of years, hundreds of thousands of jubilees, and all foreign lands are under your soles.'

The two columns of text on the back pillar, that on the right identifying Ramesses II, and that on the left identifying Amun-Ra, face each other to express communication between the king and the god. What is more, the hieroglyphs

12 Rear view of EA 19, showing the back pillar inscription.

representing the god face to the right – thus away from the temple's axis – because the god looks 'out' of his sanctuary, whereas the column representing the king faces the temple's axis, because the king is a visitor to the temple, moving in. On the back pillar of the other statue of the pair, which stood north of the temple's axis, the king's column and the the god's column would have been swapped accordingly.

The throne of the statue bears inscriptions as well.

Front of the throne near the king's right leg:

The [true] god, Lord of the Two Lands, Usermaatra-Setepenra, Son of Ra, Lord of Crowns, Ramesses-Meryamun, beloved of Amun, endowed with life.

Front of the throne near the right leg (this speech appears twice, above each of the two Nile gods):

Words spoken: '[I] accomplished the act of reuniting (Upper and Lower Egypt) for you and your father Ra, and all foreign lands are under your soles.'

Most of the inscription on the left side of the throne is destroyed, except for two cartouches of Ramesses II. However, enough remains to determine that both sides were decorated with the same scene, and presumably with the same captions to the Nile figures.

While giving a distinct identity to the statue, these inscriptions would only have been legible to a minority of the population, since the vast majority of Egyptians were illiterate. Those privileged few able to understand the hieroglyphs shared those words with a divine audience of gods whom the inscriptions invoked, and who therefore were able to appreciate the projected glory and power of 'Ramesses the Great' for themselves.

2 Creating the colossus

In most periods of Egyptian history, the state had a monopoly on access to hard stones, metals, precious woods and ivory, since they were difficult to obtain and therefore costly. Royal control of sculpture production ensured that cult statues and temple decoration could be made in abundance for the gods, whom the pharaoh represented on Earth, and royal statues were intended as monumental receptacles of the king's *ka*. While inherently valuable, certain materials were also given symbolic attributes; for example, gold was associated with the

13 Granite quarries at Aswan showing the so-called 'Unfinished Obelisk'.

skin of the gods and silver with their bones, while turquoise was linked with fertility and was sacred to the goddess Hathor. Granodiorite, as well as symbolising (pronounced 'Kemet'), the fertile black land of the Nile floodplain, was linked with the underworld and the god Osiris. These characteristics influenced the type of material chosen for a statue, which would subsequently embody those particular elements.

Granite, such as that chosen for the Ramesses statue, and quartzite were stones with solar associations. From the earliest dynasties, granite was one of the most highly valued stones, and was quarried throughout the pharaonic period. Granite was known to the ancient Egyptians as (pronounced 'maatch en abu'), meaning 'red granite of Elephantine (Aswan)'. The granite used for the statue was acquired from the Aswan area in southern Egypt, a vast quarry region around 20 square kilometres in area, where granite has been obtained from ancient times through to the present day.[2] Termed 'Variety 2 granite' by experts,[3] the medium- to fine-grained stone used for the statue varies in colour between a light grey, pink and red.[4] It was rarely used during the New Kingdom, except for sculpture. It was processed much less frequently than the characteristic 'monumental pink' granite ('Variety 1'), which was favoured for buildings and architectural features, including obelisks.[5] The precise source at Aswan of the variety of granite used for the Ramesses statue is yet to be discovered. It may have been quarried away for the construction of the Aswan Low Dam in 1902. We do know that Variety 2 occurred as thin veins running through the 'monumental pink' granite and Aswan granodiorite, which may explain why its use was limited: it would have been difficult to obtain suitable fracture-free blocks.

14 Tapered chisel used for stoneworking. Copper-alloy. From Thebes. New Kingdom (1550–1069 BC). Length 12.7 cm.

15 (overleaf) Drawing board with a draughtsman's study on one side showing a seated figure of a king within a grid, which was used to get the correct proportions. Wood. From Thebes. 18th Dynasty (1550–1295 BC). Height 53.4 cm.

Making a statue

Granite is a very hard stone, measuring between 6 and 7 on the Mohs Hardness Scale (roughly equivalent to glass or iron pyrite). Yet the technology that allowed the Egyptians to effectively work such hard stones was developed during the earliest stages of Egyptian history. Granite was worked with

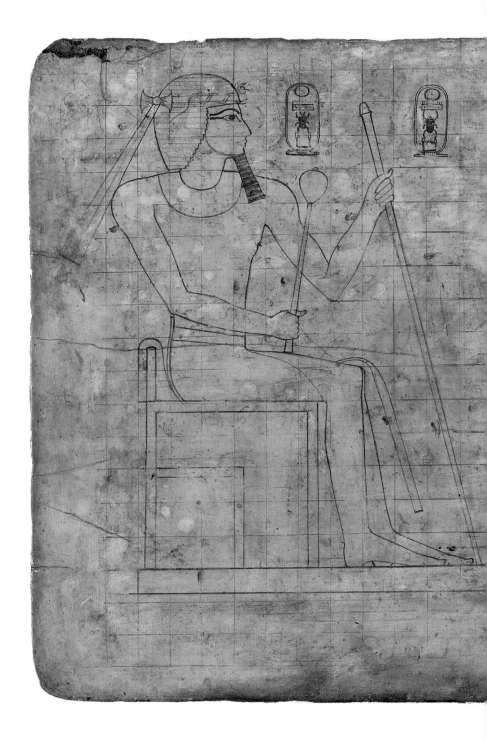

24

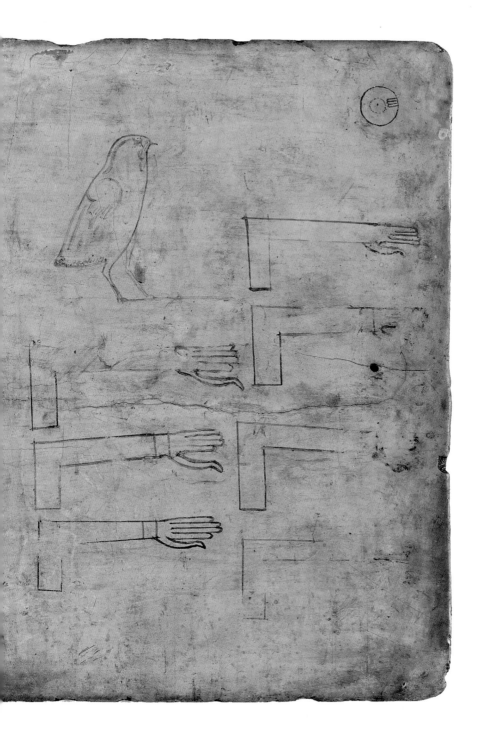

16 Unfinished statue of an enthroned female figure. Basalt. Late Period (747–332 BC). Height 30.5 cm.

hard stone hammers and copper or bronze drills, using desert sand as an abrasive, from at least the Old Kingdom (2686–2181 BC). The creation of a colossal granite statue was a delicate task: it was cut from a single block of stone which had to be quarried, transported down the Nile and finely sculpted before – or after – being erected in the temple. The Aswan granite quarries were some 200 kilometres south of the Ramesseum, reflecting the considerable organization and teamwork required to transport such a statue to Thebes.

A team of sculptors cut the statue from a single piece. Once a suitable block had been identified in the quarry, the external weathered layer of stone was removed using dolerite hammers. A two-dimensional grid and outline were then drawn on each side of the stone block in accordance with the Egyptian canon of artistic representation: a technique evident from drawn grids preserved on unfinished statuary, and also used for two-dimensional representations. The contours were roughed out with stone tools: as each layer was gradually shaped, important points were marked on the stone with dots of paint to preserve the outline as the grid was cut away.

In choosing where to position the body within the block, the sculptor appears to have deliberately exploited the bichrome nature of the stone by cutting the head from fine pink granite and the rest of the statue from darker, coarser Aswan granodiorite, with a lighter vein of pink granite dividing the two. This is also a characteristic of other examples of New Kingdom sculpture made from this variety of granite. On initial inspection it seems that the lighter vein of stone was chosen to make the statue more aesthetically pleasing, perhaps to emphasize the division between the body and the face. However, this distinction may not have been obvious to an ancient visitor to the Ramesseum, since parts of the statue, if not the whole thing, were painted and perhaps also gilded.

The shaped block was then moved onto wooden sledges and pulled by a team of workers towards the Nile, where it was loaded onto a river barge and sailed downstream to Thebes. On arrival the stone would have been transferred

17 Early 20th-century watercolour by Nina de Garis Davies of a painted wall panel from the New Kingdom tomb of Rekhmire at Thebes (TT100) showing the manufacture of a statue.

onto another wooden sledge and dragged to the Ramesseum, or floated if the Nile was in flood.

Whether or not the fine details were achieved at the quarry before the statue was moved, however, remains unclear. A depiction of a colossal statue at the quarry in Aswan dating to the reign of Amenhotep III shows a finished statue named 'Ruler of Rulers', which may suggest that it was mostly finished at the quarry before being transported. However, the image may have been made

27

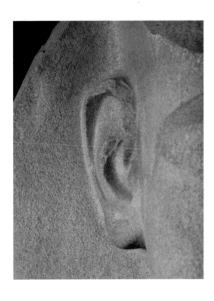

18 Detail of the statue's right ear, showing surviving traces of red and yellow pigment on the face and crown.

retrospectively, and may simply illustrate a complete object that was actually unfinished when it left the quarry, since it would have been unwise to transport such large statues in a fully finished state. A degree of rough handling would certainly have affected the carved details. Similarly, whether colossi were quarried and transported on their side and then raised *in situ* at the temple, as an obelisk would have been, remains uncertain; but this method is suggested by grooves preserved on the bases of some examples, including the famous 'Colossi of Memnon' (see pages 30–31). A well-known depiction of the transportation of a Middle Kingdom (2055–1650 BC) seated colossus in the tomb of the governor Djehutyhotep at Deir el-Bersha appears to show that the statue, in its finished form, was actually transported in an upright position. The extent to which this reflects artistic convention is unknown, but the size of the statue as suggested by the image may also be misleading. Artistic decorum dictated that the tomb owner, in this instance shown by the statue, be depicted on a larger scale than the other figures in a scene.

Surviving plaster and colour on the surface of some hard-stone statues indicate that they were originally painted using natural pigments, including ochre for yellow and red, carbon for black, and gypsum for white. Particular features, such as clothing, may have been painted and the remainder, perhaps the skin, left unpainted. Traces of red pigment remain on the head and torso of the statue, and on the head of the northern statue. Traces of black (for the eye pupils) and blue and yellow (for the stripes of the headcloth) also remain on the head, while traces of red and yellow can also be seen on the cobra crown, and red painted bands on the broad collar. For stones such as granite and quartzite, highly polished areas such as the skin contrasted with deliberately roughened areas, here the crown, eyebrows and false beard, which provided an effective surface for pigment or gilding.

3 Living images: the power and purpose of colossal sculpture

... the acceptance of the material as a means of conveying the relationship between human-lived biological time and the aeons of geological time is an essential condition of the waiting quality of sculpture.

ANTHONY GORMLEY, SCULPTOR[6]

Although physically human, the pharaoh was acknowledged as a living god; an embodiment of the royal *ka*-spirit who acted as mediator between the human and divine worlds. Distinct royal identities for these pharaohs were fashioned through the creation of colossal statues. These statues were intended to act as an alternative home for the royal *ka*, while also advertising the pharaoh's power and piety to both gods and men, and facilitating the magical participation of the *ka* in the regular rituals established before and after the death of the king. Pharaonic statues embodied the belief that both human and divine spirits needed to be housed, appeased and nurtured within specific vessels, each forming a permanent, physical body for these spirits. The statues also emphasized the equivalence of pharaohs and divinities, and had an important audience among the gods themselves. Pharaohs used the medium of colossal sculpture to make themselves as visible and enduring as possible, in the hope of ensuring a successful reign: they were eager to be seen as strong, capable leaders. Royal statues, erected throughout Egypt, allowed the pharaoh to be perpetually present in all of Egypt's temples, no matter where he might be in reality. Both royal and private statues were vitalized through the 'opening of the mouth' ritual, when special tools magically activated the senses to enable the statue to receive the spirit of the pharaoh. The statues themselves were not considered to be alive, but the spirits inhabiting them were, and as such they could receive prayers and offerings.

Seated colossal statues in pairs commonly flanked temple entrances to symbolically protect the sacred inner space of the temple. They received offerings as focal points of cult

19 (above) Seated colossal quartzite statues of Amenhotep III, known as the 'Colossi of Memnon', which mark the now-lost entrance to his memorial temple on the West Bank at Thebes.

worship in their own right, as the interface between those with restricted access to the outer parts of the temple, and the less accessible sacred area occupied by the gods within. Colossi were, in principle, foci of popular worship, on a daily basis or on festival occasions, though it is difficult to determine the precise nature of this interaction. Examples of individuals shown worshipping these statues can be seen on the 'Horbeit Stelae', a group of stelae found in Qantir but likely originally from nearby Piramesse. These stelae depict individually named colossal statues as figures of worship and embodiments of the divine essence of the king, in much the same way as the statues of the gods were worshipped.

Particular colossal statues appear to have received worship in their own right, distinct from any other divine cult; there is evidence for this during the reigns of both Amenhotep III and Ramesses II. This is especially clear at the temple of Amenhotep III at Soleb in Nubia, where the pharaoh wished to represent his divine element as a distinct entity called 'Amenhotep Lord of Nubia'. However, he also wished to be represented as a living person who is shown offering to his divine self on the walls of the temple; a practice which has been dubbed 'auto-adoration'.[7] These colossi depicted on the temple walls were also named: each name including that of the pharaoh alongside additional elements such as 'Ra-of-Rulers' and 'Ruler of Rulers'. The names were shown both within a cartouche and without a cartouche, which may illustrate the particular emphasis on the living aspect of kingship (with a cartouche), and the divine aspect of kingship (without). Through the act of naming the colossi, the distinction of their particular identities may have made it easier for the living audiences to appeal to particular statues, while also ensuring that they remained cult objects throughout the reign and after the death of the king.

20 (right) Line drawing of a 'Horbeit Stela', probably originally from the site of Qantir. It shows the king's butler, called Ramessu-men, giving offerings to two statues of Ramesses II.

Before Ramesses II, the production of colossal statuary is especially well known for the reign of Amenhotep III;

most recognizably by the 'Colossi of Memnon', which indicate the position of the lost entrance to his once-vast memorial temple on the West Bank at Thebes. Ramesses' commitment to the production of colossal statuary was perhaps an attempt to associate himself with, and to emulate the accomplishments of, Amenhotep III, who was a prolific builder and producer of sculpture and the last orthodox ruler before the Amarna Period.[8] The Amarna Period is the name given by Egyptologists to the rule of the heretic pharaoh Akhenaten, who temporarily abolished the worship of the traditional Egyptian gods in favour of a monotheistic religion focused on the sun disc, the Aten, and built a new capital at Amarna. After Akhenaten's death the old religion was brought back and there were strenuous attempts to expunge this aberrant episode from the historical record. Ramesses is known to have usurped sculpture originally produced for Amenhotep III by reshaping the features and changing the names of the statues.

The great challenge of quarrying, transporting and working hard stones for colossal statues meant that it was common anyhow for pharaohs to reuse existing sculpture in their own building programmes. This was especially true of kings who chose to build in the Delta, which lacked local hard-stone quarries. For example, the kings of the 21st Dynasty transported colossi and architectural elements of Ramesses II from Piramesse to Tanis and Bubastis, where they were re-inscribed and re-erected in new temples. Rather than an attempt to deliberately obliterate Ramesses' monumental legacy, this was an economical measure designed to cut costs. Although Ramesses is well known for recutting and re-inscribing statues of his predecessors, there is no indication that the British Museum's statue was usurped from a previous ruler.

Royal power at Egypt's boundaries

The divine aspect of the pharaoh was also made visible at the periphery of Egypt, expressed formally through the construction of royal temples. Nubia was gradually reconquered from the beginning of the New Kingdom in

21 (overleaf)
Façade of the Great
Temple of Abu Simbel
with four colossal
seated statues of
Ramesses II.

1550 BC: pharaohs campaigned further and further along the Nile and established new towns and temples at strategic locations. Ramesses created a series of rock-cut temples in Nubia, of which the Great Temple of Abu Simbel is the most grandiose, and it gives us the best sense of how colossal statues would have appeared in the landscape. It was dedicated to the gods Ra-Horakhty, Amun and Ptah, as well as the deified Ramesses himself. Ramesses chose to make the entire exterior of the temple a colossal memorial to himself in his own image: four 21-metre-high rock-cut seated statues mark the entrance to the temple, as unmistakable markers of the pharaoh's power over foreign lands and as a mediator of access to the divine. This temple, which may have influenced the design of the rock-cut faces of the American presidents at Mount Rushmore, was famously relocated to high ground during the creation of the Aswan Dam in the 1960s to prevent it becoming submerged by Lake Nasser. These colossal memorials projected the royal power and divinity of the pharaoh, impressing ancient visitors to the temple, Classical authors and generations of modern visitors to Egypt.

4 A monumental challenge: Salt, Belzoni and the British Museum

Classical encounters

The Ramesseum featured on the journey through Egypt undertaken by ancient Greek travellers. The oldest surviving description of the colossal statue of Ramesses was made by the classical historian Diodorus Siculus, a contemporary of Julius Caesar, in the first century BC. In his *Bibliotheca Historica* he called the Ramesseum the 'Tomb of Osymandyas'. His use of the term 'Osymandyas' was a Hellenized rendering of the first element of Ramesses' *prenomen* or throne-name: Usermaatra, meaning 'Ra is powerful of truth'. In his travel account Diodorus describes two statues in the second courtyard of the Ramesseum and provides his translation of one of the statue inscriptions:

> I am Osymandyas, king of kings; if any one wishes to know who I am and where I lie, let him surpass me in some of my exploits.[9]

The epithet 'king of kings' could refer to an inscription on the upper-right arm of the toppled red granite colossus at the Ramesseum that preserves the cartouche of Usermaatra 'Sun of Princes', which can also be read as 'king of kings'. However, Diodorus' account of the Ramesseum may be fictional in part since he seemingly did not travel as far south as Thebes, and may instead have based his version, and this translation, on descriptions by others, which are now lost.

Classical visitors, including the Greek historian Strabo, mistakenly named the site the 'Memnonium' after the mythical Ethiopian king Memnon. The two colossal seated statues of Amenhotep III at the entrance of his memorial temple in Thebes, cut from single pieces of quartzite, were similarly named the 'Colossi of Memnon' by Classical visitors who also equated them with the mythical Memnon. As a result the statue of Ramesses II was subsequently dubbed the 'Younger Memnon' by nineteenth-century travellers; a name by which it is still known today.

European encounters

The Ramesseum has long been favoured as a travel destination by Western explorers and writers. The English traveller Richard Pococke (1704–65) visited the Ramesseum during a tour of Egypt in 1737 and in his account, *A Description of the East* (1743), included several images of the temple, one of which appears to include the intact colossus. Frederick Ludwig Norden (1708–42), a captain in the Danish Navy and an early traveller to Egypt, also visited the Ramesseum in 1737–8, providing illustrations and a description of the site in his account *Voyage d'Égypte et de Nubie* (1755). In this text he noted that the colossus had fallen but was still intact at that time, facing downwards and partially buried in the sand; a position reflected in the contemporary colloquial name given to the statue by locals: el-Kafany, meaning 'one who is overthrown'.

The Scottish traveller and writer James Bruce (1730–94) spent more than a decade in Africa in an attempt to trace the origins of the Nile, and visited the Ramesseum in the 1760s, later including the colossus in his *Travels to Discover the Source of the Nile* (1790). The Napoleonic expedition to Egypt visited the Ramesseum in 1799 and meticulously documented the site for inclusion in the encyclopaedic *Description de l'Égypte* (1809–22) and in the account of the savant Dominique Vivant Denon (1747–1825), *Voyages dans la basse et la haute Égypte* (1802).

The Napoleonic expedition put the Ramesseum firmly on the map of European travellers, and as such the site regularly featured in travel accounts, including that of the British traveller and diplomat William Richard Hamilton (1777–1859) who visited Egypt after the Napoleonic invasion. He vividly described the statue in his *Aegyptiaca* of 1809:

> It is certainly the most beautiful and perfect piece of Egyptian sculpture that can be seen throughout the whole country. We were struck by its extraordinary delicacy; the very uncommon expression visible in its features ...[10]

Jean François Champollion (1790–1832), the Frenchman who finally deciphered the hieroglyphic script, visited the

22 (previous pages) Engraving of the Ramesseum by the Napoleonic expedition to Egypt, entitled 'Vue du péristyle du tombeau and des débris de la statue colossale d'Osymandyas, prise de l'ouest' (View of the peristyle of the tomb and the debris of the colossal statue of Osymandyas, taken from the west).

Ramesseum in 1829 and correctly identified the temple as that of Ramesses II after translating a cartouche at the site. The *Description de l'Égypte* records that the statue had been broken into two pieces, perhaps by an explosion, by the time of the Napoleonic visit to the Ramesseum. We cannot know with certainty the cause of this damage – whether human or natural. The Napoleonic party themselves have been accused: during his tour of Upper Egypt in 1813, the Swiss explorer Johann Ludwig Burckhardt (1784–1817) was informed by local villagers on the West Bank at Thebes that the French were responsible for the damage, and William Hamilton also cited the French as the likely perpetrators in his *Aegyptiaca*. A hole bored through the chest of the statue, around 5 centimetres in diameter, remains clearly visible; the statue was described by Salt and Burckhardt as 'having on one of its shoulders a hole bored artificially, supposed to have been made by the French for separating the fragment of the body'; a defining feature which would help Belzoni identify the statue (see page 45 below). However, whether it was indeed the French who made this hole in a botched attempt to separate the head from the body, and therefore make it more easily transportable, has since been questioned; it could well have happened before the Napoleonic visit. Whoever was responsible for the damage did not harm the striking face, which meant that the statue was a great attraction for collectors who considered it ripe for the picking.

The British Museum

During the nineteenth century the British Museum's Egyptian collection grew significantly from one consisting mainly of easily portable 'curiosity' pieces collected by early travellers, to one more representative of the range of Egyptian artistic traditions. Following the defeat of Napoleon's armies in Egypt on 2 September 1801, the French surrendered to the British and Turkish armies and were obliged to consent to the Treaty of Alexandria, which stated that all of the Egyptian antiquities collected by the French during their campaign were to be considered public property. This collection included statues, sarcophagi and the Rosetta Stone, which subsequently proved the key to deciphering hieroglyphs. The items were presented to King George III (r. 1760–1820) who then gifted them to the British Museum. They were added to the Museum's collection in 1802 and the Townley Gallery was subsequently opened in 1808 to accommodate the expanding collection. The Egyptian Room was the largest of all the new exhibition spaces in the Townley Gallery; this meant that for the first time the Egyptian collection could stand alone as a highlight of the Museum's antiquities collection, not just as a collection of curiosities. At this time, however, Egyptian antiquities were viewed as aesthetically inferior to Classical works and relatively little was known about the objects because the hieroglyphic script had yet to be deciphered. The gallery thus lacked any distinct themes, and objects were presented as *objets d'art* without any meaningful reference to their date or original context, since the chronology of ancient Egyptian history was yet to be written.

The war of the Consuls

The new Egyptian sculpture gallery generated a great deal of interest, since nothing like it had ever been seen in London before. Visitors were fascinated by the monumental statues and the mysterious ancient hieroglyphs which covered them. The British Museum was eager to collect as many inscribed ancient Egyptian objects as possible; the determination of British scholars to beat their French rivals to the goal of successfully deciphering the hieroglyphic script lent the mission a sense of added urgency. However, the British Museum was made to compete for objects with the French consul, Bernardino Drovetti (1776–1852), who had already amassed a fine collection of Egyptian antiquities which he exported for sale in Europe, much of which formed the nucleus of the Egyptian Museum in Turin. The British Consul in Egypt was Henry Salt (1780–1827) who, soon after entering office in March 1816, began to supplement his income through the collection and sale of Egyptian antiquities. At that time, individual Europeans were discouraged from excavating ancient sites, but in contrast consular agents were given *carte blanche* to collect and export Egyptian objects. The British Museum secured its status as a

23 The British Consul in Egypt, Henry Salt. Stipple engraving after a portrait by John James Halls, 1827 or after.

centre for Egyptian antiquities following the acquisition of monumental sculptures from Salt's First Collection, many of which were collected by his agent in Egypt, the Italian excavator Giovanni Battista Belzoni (1778–1823).

The 'Patagonian Sampson'

Belzoni had performed for many years in London as a theatrical showman, known as the 'Patagonian Sampson'. He was unusually tall at 6 feet 8 inches (over 2 metres), with strong, handsome features, and during his time in London he appeared on stage at Sadler's Wells Theatre, where he also gained practical knowledge of water mechanics from the production of stage sets. In 1815 Belzoni moved to Cairo

24 Portrait of Giovanni Battista Belzoni. Stipple engraving by James Thompson, 1822, after a portrait by an unknown artist.

where the then ruler (pasha) Muhammad Ali (1769–1849) heard of his experience with hydraulics and employed him to assist in the creation of a new form of waterwheel to boost the development of Egypt's water resources. Belzoni duly created his prototype within three or four months but Muhammad Ali was unimpressed with Belzoni's ideas and ejected him from the project in 1816.

After this disappointment, in 1816 Belzoni approached Johann Ludwig Burckhardt, with whom he was already acquainted, to discuss the possibility of removing the colossal statue of Ramesses to the British Museum. Burckhardt had been considering this for some time – since he first saw the statue and attempted to convince Muhammad Ali to send it

as a gift to England. However, in the eyes of the pasha, stone
was not an appropriate diplomatic gift, even when worked
to such a high standard. Through Burckhardt, Belzoni
was subsequently introduced to Henry Salt, and from
that moment Salt and Belzoni commenced a productive
campaign of imperial power on behalf of the new British
consulate: removing Egyptian sculpture to be transported to
England with the full support of the pasha.

Acquisition
In 1816 Belzoni arrived, with the following letter of
instruction from Salt and Burckhardt:

> Mr. Belzoni is requested to prepare the necessary
> implements, at Boulak, for the purpose of raising
> the head of the statue of the Younger Memnon and
> carrying it down the Nile. He will proceed as speedily as
> circumstances will allow to Siout [Asyut], there to deliver
> his letters prepared for that effect, to Ibrahim Pacha, or
> whoever may be left in the charge of the government,
> and he will at that place consult with Dr. Scotto [Ibrahim
> Pasha's personal physician] on the subject of his further
> proceedings. He will take care to engage a proper boat
> for bringing down the head, and will request Dr. Scotto
> to provide him with a soldier to go up with him for the
> purpose of engaging the fellahs [labourers] to work when
> he may require their aid, as otherwise they are not likely
> to attend to Mr. Belzoni's orders, and he should on no
> account leave Siout without an interpreter.
>
> Having obtained the necessary permission to hire
> workmen, Mr. Belzoni will proceed direct to Thebes.
> He will find the Head referred to on the Western side
> of the river, opposite to Carnac [the Temple of Amun,
> Karnak, Thebes], in the vicinity of a village called
> Gournou [Qurna], lying on the southern side of a ruined
> temple [the Ramesseum] called by the natives Kossar
> el Deka'ki. To the head is still attached a portion of the
> shoulders, so that altogether it is of large dimensions,
> and will be recognized – 1st by circumstance lying on its
> back, with the face uppermost – 2nd by the face being

quite perfect and very beautiful – 3rdly by having on one of its shoulders a hole bored artificially, supposed to have been made by the French for separating the fragment of the body – and 4thly, from its being of a mixed blackish and reddish granite, and covered with Hieroglyphics on its shoulders. It must not be mistaken for another [the northern statue of the pair at the Ramesseum] lying in that neighbourhood, which is <u>much mutilated</u>.

Mr. Belzoni will spare no expense or trouble in getting it as speedily conveyed to the bank of the river as possible; and he will, if it be necessary, let it await there till the river has attained sufficient height before he attempts to get it into the Boat. But at the same time, he is requested not to attempt removing it, on any account, if he should judge there to be any risk of either injuring the Head, or burying the face in the sand, or of losing it in the Nile.

If, on arriving at the ground, too, he should perceive that his means are inadequate, or that the difficulties of the undertaking, from the nature of the ground, or other causes, are likely to prove insurmountable, he will at once relinquish the enterprize [sic], and not enter into further expense on that account.

Mr. Belzoni will have the goodness to keep a separate account of the expenses incurred in this undertaking, which, as well as his other expenses, will gladly be reimbursed; as, from the knowledge of Mr. Belzoni's character, it is confidently believed they will be as reasonable as circumstances will allow.

The boat meant to carry the head should be hired for a sufficient time to allow of its being carried directly down to Alexandria, but on the way, Mr. Belzoni will not fail to stop at Boulak for further instructions.

If Mr. Belzoni should ascertain the certainty of his being able to accomplish his purpose, he is requested immediately to despatch an express with the gratifying intelligence to Cairo.[11]

(Signed) HENRY SALT
SHEIKH IBRAHIM [J. L. BURCKHARDT]

The instructions were straightforward: Belzoni should undertake to remove the statue from the Ramesseum and he should keep a record of all his expenses in order to be reimbursed, while being permitted to abandon the challenge if it should prove too difficult. Previous attempts to move the statue had failed, including that by the British traveller and collector William John Bankes (1786–1855) who unsuccessfully took ropes and pulleys to the site during his visit in 1815.

Thus commenced Belzoni's mission to remove the statue and transport it first to the river's edge, and then along the Nile to Alexandria, from where it would be transferred to England. Time was of the essence as Belzoni had to take advantage of the rising water level during the annual Nile inundation in order to move the statue; should the operation take too long the water would cover the land between the temple and the river and perhaps even submerge the stranded statue.

Belzoni left Cairo for Luxor in 1816 with a hired interpreter and dragoman, Giovanni d'Athanasi, and on seeing the statue remarked that the face was:

> … apparently smiling on me, at the thought of being taken to England.[12]

By late July 1816 Belzoni had removed the statue from the Ramesseum with the help of a workforce of local men recruited from the nearby village of Qurna, and on 12 August it had arrived by the West Bank of the Nile at Luxor. The equipment comprised fourteen wooden beams, four lengths of palm rope and four logs upon which the statue was rolled to the riverbank, in a manner not dissimilar to the ancient transportation of the stone. Belzoni's own account of the work was somewhat self-dramatizing:

> By means of four levers I raised the statue, so as to leave a vacancy under it, to introduce the car; and after it was slowly lodged on this, I had the car raised in the front, with the statue on it, so as to get one of

the rollers underneath. I then had the same operation performed at the back, and the colossus was ready to be pulled up. I caused it to be well secured on the car, and the ropes so placed that the power might be divided. I stationed men with levers at each side of the car, to assist occasionally if the colossus should be inclined to turn to either side. In this manner I kept it safe from falling. Lastly, I placed men in the front, distributing them equally at the four ropes, while others were ready to change the rollers alternately. Thus I succeeded in getting it removed the distance of several yards from its original place. According to my instructions, I sent an Arab to Cairo with the intelligence that the statue had begun its journey towards England.[13]

Belzoni's relationship with the local workmen was not without problems: on 6 August they stopped working for Belzoni, owing to Drovetti's influence over the local administrator, who was a personal acquaintance. With the Nile waters close to flooding, Belzoni immediately visited the office of the administrator and threatened him at gunpoint until he was able to rehire the workmen to complete the job. On 15 November Belzoni recruited 130 local men to help make a causeway to facilitate the movement of the head from the Nile bank down to the riverside. The statue was safely loaded onto a river barge, arriving in Cairo on 15 December 1816.

Belzoni immortalized his great feat of engineering in a coloured lithograph and emphatically described the movement of the statue onto the boat:

I succeeded in my attempt and the head of the younger Memnon was actually embarked. I cannot help observing that it was no easy undertaking to put a piece of granite of such bulk and weight on board a boat that, if it received the weight on one side, would immediately upset. … The causeway I had made gradually sloped to the edge of the water close to the boat, and with the four poles I formed a bridge from the bank into the centre of the boat so that when the

25 Coloured lithograph entitled 'Mode in Which the Young Memnon Head Now in the British Museum was Removed' by Giovanni Battista Belzoni, 1816.

weight bore on the bridge, it pressed only on the centre of the boat. The bridge rested partly on the causeway, partly on the side of the boat, and partly on this centre of it. On the opposite side of the boat I put some mats well filled with straw. I necessarily stationed a few Arabs in the boat, and some at each side, with a lever of palm wood, as I had nothing else. At the middle of the bridge I put a sack filled with sand that, if the colossus should run too fast into the boat, it might be stopped. In the ground behind the colossus I had a piece of palm tree firmly planted, round which a rope was twisted and then fastened to its car to let it descend gradually. I set a lever at work on each side, and at the same time that the men in the boat were pulling, others were slackening ropes, and others shifting the rollers as the colossus advanced.[14]

The statue was successfully moved to Rosetta and finally
to the port of Alexandria on 14 January 1817. It lay in one
of Muhammad Ali's warehouses on a pier until October
1817, by which time the British Museum and the Foreign
Office had arranged for a British naval vessel to move
the statue onwards to Malta. After the usual period in
quarantine in Malta the statue travelled on the ship *Weymouth*
to England, where it arrived in March 1818. London's
Quarterly Review announced that Henry Salt's first shipment
of Egyptian objects was en route to the British Museum in
January 1818, describing the statue as:

> ... without doubt the finest specimen of ancient
> Egyptian sculpture which has yet been discovered.[15]

26 (above) Graffiti of Belzoni and Salt in the hypostyle hall of the Ramesseum.

27 (opposite) Sketch by William Alexander of the installation of the statue of Ramesses in the Townley Gallery on 9 January 1819. Soldiers of the Royal Engineers use heavy ropes and lifting equipment under the watchful eye of Major Charles Cornwallis Dansey.

In spite of the challenges inherent in such an undertaking, including those of diplomacy, negotiation, extortion, and international customs and excise, Belzoni succeeded in his mission and the statue was presented as a gift to the British Museum by Salt and Burckhardt in November 1818, though Belzoni's name was omitted from the official donation. Belzoni only removed the upper part of the statue; the base still stands in the Ramesseum and upon it is preserved the graffito *Belzoni 1816*. Belzoni's name is also preserved in small, neat letters on the rear section of the crown of cobras on the statue in the British Museum. Belzoni and Salt also left their names on a wall in the Ramesseum's hypostyle hall, with Belzoni's being much larger and deeper-cut than that of Salt.

Installation

The statue was installed in the Egyptian Room of the Townley Gallery of the British Museum on 9 January 1819, dwarfing the existing arrangement. The process of installation was a major feat of engineering. Owing to the

immense weight of the Ramesses statue, the assistance of the Army's Royal Engineers was required to move it into the new gallery. A description of the statue's installation can be found in the *Gentleman's Magazine* of January to June 1819:

> The Head of Memnon, sent to England by Mr. [Henry] Salt ... has been recently placed, most judiciously as to light,

on a pedestal in the Egyptian Room in the British Museum, under the able direction of Mr. [Taylor] Combe. We congratulate the public on this valuable acquisition, which may perhaps be considered as the most perfect specimen of Egyptian art in the world. On entering the room the immensity of the Head has its full effect on the spectator, when seen in the same view with the famous figure of the Discobulus [sic], which is the size of life, and stands at a short distance from it. From the proportion of the features it may be concluded that the figure, when perfect, was about twenty feet in height. The Head has suffered a loss of part of the right side of its skull, yet the features are all entire. They are truly beautiful, partaking more of the Grecian than of the Egyptian character, and are as sharp and perfect as when they were left by the chisel. Although the Head represents a young person, yet it has a long beard.[16]

The challenge faced by the Museum was to transform the statue from a 'curiosity' to an object fit to be included in the existing Classical arrangement: a difficult task, since very little of the historical context of the statue was known at that time. Following its installation in the British Museum, the statue was studied in detail by G. H. Noeden, a sub-librarian at the Museum, who attempted to bridge the gap between the object as a curiosity and the object as an artefact, while including accurate measurements of the piece – perhaps in an attempt to find a link between the Egyptian statue and Classical Graeco-Roman proportions. The British Museum guidebooks then began to describe the statue in aesthetic terms, with George Long even commenting in the 1832 Guidebook that '... the nostrils of the Memnon are, in our opinion, the finest pair in all the Museum'.

Unfortunately for Henry Salt his gift was not as well received by the Museum as he had anticipated, and the Trustees failed to acknowledge the donors for their gesture. During the installation, the Director of the British Museum, Joseph Banks, relayed the following message to Salt:

> Though in truth we are here much satisfied with the
> Memnon, and consider it as a chef-d'oeuvre of Egyptian

sculpture, yet we have not placed that statue among the works of Fine Art. It stands in the Egyptian Rooms. Whether any statue that has been found in Egypt can be brought into competition with the grand [classical] works of the Townley Gallery remains to be proved unless however they really are so, the prices you have set upon your acquisitions are very unlikely to be realized in Europe.[17]

Despite this comment, not long after the statue arrived Salt offered the British Museum the opportunity to purchase his important collection of Egyptian antiquities, which included many objects acquired by Belzoni in Egypt, such as the calcite sarcophagus of Sety I from his tomb in the Valley of the Kings. The collection was finally purchased by the British Museum for £2,000, significantly less than Salt had expected. The Sety I sarcophagus was purchased separately by the architect and collector Sir John Soane (1753–1837), in whose museum at Lincoln's Inn Fields it resides today.

The growth of all areas of the British Museum's collection resulted in a need to increase gallery space and led to the construction of the Smirke Egyptian Sculpture Gallery, which was completed in 1851; this is at the heart of the building currently occupied by the Museum on Great Russell Street.

In this new gallery the objects were presented in chronological order with objects facing inwards down the length of the gallery; an arrangement made possible by Champollion's decipherment of hieroglyphs in 1822. The statue was displayed alongside the colossal granite fist of Ramesses II (EA 9) and a cast of one of the colossal heads of Ramesses II from his temple at Abu Simbel. Between 1851 and 1981, the objects in the Sculpture Gallery were subsequently reorganized into smaller groups, displayed in a more contextual arrangement rather than as isolated *objets d'art*. Building on this, a major redisplay of the gallery in 1981 positioned the Ramesses statue at something like its original height at the Ramesseum, where it can be seen today, looming over all those who walk by.

Ozymandias

'Ozymandias' is … more than a poem about an object. It is an instance of how in the emergent institutions of Egyptology and Egyptomania there was no important difference between stories and materials.

E. COLLA, 2007[18]

It is often assumed that the installation of the statue in the Townley Gallery inspired the English poet Percy Bysshe Shelley (1792–1822) to write his sonnet 'Ozymandias' in 1817. This work was described by John Rodenbeck in a 2004 article as 'one of the greatest and most famous poems in the English language'.[19]

> I met a traveller from an antique land
> Who said: "Two vast and trunkless legs of stone
> Stand in the desert. Near them on the sand,
> Half sunk, a shattered visage lies, whose frown
> And wrinkled lip and sneer of cold command
> Tell that its sculptor well those passions read
> Which yet survive, stamped on these lifeless things,
> The hand that mocked them and the heart that fed.
> And on the pedestal these words appear:
> 'My name is Ozymandias, king of kings:
> Look on my works, ye mighty, and despair!'
> Nothing beside remains. Round the decay
> Of that colossal wreck, boundless and bare,
> The lone and level sands stretch far away."[20]

Under the pseudonym Glirastes, Shelley published this poem in Leigh Hunt's *The Examiner* on 11 January 1818, having written the sonnet in late 1817. The journey of the statue from Egypt to England was widely documented in the European press and, being inspired by the story, friendly rivalry between Shelley and his fellow poet Horace Smith (1779–1849) led each of them to write and publish a poem entitled 'Ozymandias'. Smith's 'Ozymandias', describing the colossal leg of a statue, was also published in *The Examiner* a fortnight later on 25 January 1818. Shelley's vivid evocation of Ozymandias in particular portrays a warning of the

28 Anonymous watercolour from February 1820 of the Egyptian Room in the Townley Gallery, showing the Ramesses statue on the right, entitled 'A Room in the Sculpture Gallery of the British Museum. From a sketch taken on the spot in February 1819'.

arrogance of great leaders, whose attempts to immortalize their own tyrannical power through sculpture succeed only in emphasizing their reprehensible passions.

The publication of the poems was undoubtedly deliberately timed to capitalize on the public interest in the arrival of Salt's collection of Egyptian antiquities. However, the idea that Shelley received direct inspiration from the object seems to be a suitably Romantic myth, as he published the poem before the statue had even arrived in England. It therefore simply cannot be the case that he was inspired after seeing the statue for himself, and there is also no evidence to suggest that Shelley had previously visited the Ramesseum to see the statue *in situ*. The ship carrying the statue docked in England in March 1818, at least two months after the publication of 'Ozymandias', and in the same month in

29 Nineteenth-century engraving by William Radclyffe of the Smirke Egyptian Sculpture Gallery, with the Ramesses statue on the left, showing a more contextual display of objects.

which Shelley and his household permanently relocated to Italy. Shelley's 'wrinkled lip and sneer of cold command' also contrasts strongly with the rounded, almost smiling facial features of the statue. Instead, it can be safely assumed that both Shelley and Smith were influenced by a long tradition of travel writing and existing descriptions of the statue, and of the Ramesseum, in the press and from sources including Diodorus Siculus, Pococke and Denon, and perhaps also from the Napoleonic *Description de l'Égypte*. Indeed, the 'traveller from an antique land' mentioned in Shelley's opening line may have been William Richard Hamilton, whose travel account *Aegyptiaca* would have been a tremendous inspiration for the two poets.

A more obvious source for Shelley's inspiration would be Diodorus' description of the statue. The construction 'Ozymandias, king of kings' is based on Diodorus' translation of the cartouche on the upper-right arm of the toppled red granite colossus at the Ramesseum, which preserves the name Usermaatra (= Ozymandias), 'Sun of Princes' (= king of kings). Shelley's lines echo Diodorus.

Shelley's 'Ozymandias' is probably Egyptology's most significant contribution to world literature, and its enduring impact continues to be felt. Recent political parodies comparing Ozymandias with the fall of Saddam Hussein and the Soviet Union, highlighting the destruction of statues depicting political leaders, similarly serve as commentaries on the transitory nature of earthly power.

5 'So good they named it thrice'

30 The statue today in the Egyptian Sculpture Gallery at the British Museum. The colossal statue of Ramesses sits at the heart of the current Egyptian Sculpture Gallery at the British Museum, and indeed at the heart of the Egyptian collection itself. Since Champollion's decipherment of hieroglyphs it has continued to wear its three names on museum labels: 'The Younger Memnon', Ozymandias, and the modern translation: Ramesses II.

As he once did in antiquity, Ramesses II now gazes imperiously down upon those who visit him. While he is no longer revered as a symbol of divine kingship, his majestic visage is instead appreciated by the millions of British Museum visitors annually who seek to meet his eternal stare. Ramesses, and the statue's association with Shelley's 'Ozymandias', remain a source of inspiration in popular culture; whether as the subject of caricature relating to political events, or indeed when Ramesses' mummy came alive on the occasion of its visit to Paris in 1976 – at least in the poetry of Edwin Morgan:

> (The Mummy [of Ramses II] was met at
> Orly airport by Mme Saunier-Seité.
> News item, September 1976)

> Mme. S-S: … to Ramses, to Ozymandias,
> to the Louis Quatorze of the Nile,
> how bitter it must be to feel
> a microbe eat your camphored bands.

> But we are here to help Your Majesty.
> We shall encourage you to unwind.
> You have many useful years ahead.

> Ramesses: M' n'm 'z 'zym'ndias, kng'v kngz!

> Mme. S-S: Yes, yes. Well, Shelley is dead now.
> He was not embalmed. He will not write
> About Your Majesty again.[21]

Notes

1 For more on the detailed study of the statue and the re-erection of the statue base see C. Leblanc, 'Diodore, Le Tombeau d'Osymandias et la Statuaire du Ramesseum', in P. Posener-Kriéger, (ed.), *Mélanges Gamal Eddin Mokhtar*, Cairo, 1985, and C. Leblanc & D. Esmoingt, (1999), 'Le "Jeune Memnon": Un Colosse de Ramsès II nommé "Ousermaâtre-Setepenrê aimé-d'Amon-Rê"', *Memnonia* X: 79–100 [& pls XII–XXVII].

2 R. Klemm & D. D. Klemm, *Stones and Quarries in Ancient Egypt*, 2nd edition (translated from the German), London, 2008, p. 233.

3 B. A. Aston, J. Harrell and I. Shaw, 'Stone', in I. Shaw and P. N. Nicholson, (eds), *Ancient Egyptian Materials and Technology*, Cambridge, 2000, p. 36.

4 'Variety 2' granite consists mainly of quartz, microcline, oligoclase and biotite plus minor horneblende and accessory minerals (mostly apatite, sphene, zircon and iron oxides). The colour varies according to the amount and coloration of microcline in the stone.

5 Aston et al., 'Stone'.

6 As quoted in N. MacGregor, *A History of the World in 100 Objects*, London, 2010.

7 C. Price, 'Ramesses, "King of Kings": On the Context and Interpretation of Royal Colossi', in M. Collier & S. Snape, (eds), *Ramesside Studies in Honour of K. A. Kitchen*, Bolton, 2011, p. 405.

8 M. Eaton-Krauss, 'Ramesses: Re who Creates the Gods', in R. E. Freed & E. Bleiberg, (eds), *Fragments of a Shattered Visage: Proceedings of the International Symposium on Ramesses the Great*, Memphis, Tennessee, 1991, pp. 15–23.

9 Diodorus Siculus, *Biblioteca Historica*, first century BC, chapter 47.

10 W. R. Hamilton, *Remarks on several parts of Turkey (Band 1): Aegyptiaca, or some account of the antient and modern state of Egypt, as obtained in the years 1801, 1802*, London, 1809, p. 177.

11 Department of Ancient Egypt and Sudan, The British Museum, AES Ar.235, Item 1, dated 28 June 1816. Original emphases.

12 G. B. Belzoni, *Narrative of the operations and recent discoveries within the pyramids, temples, tombs, and excavations in Egypt and Nubia: and of a journey to the coast of the Red Sea in search of the ancient Berenice, and another to the oasis of Jupiter Ammon*, London, 1820, p. 39.

13 Belzoni, *Narrative*, pp. 43–4.

14 Belzoni, *Narrative*, pp. 131–2.

15 *Quarterly Review* XVIII (1817–18), p. 368.

16 *Gentlemen's Magazine* LXXXIX (Jan.–June 1819), p. 61.

17 Joseph Banks to Henry Salt, 14 February 1819, in *The Life and Correspondence of Henry Salt, Esq.*, vol. 2, 1834, p. 303.

18 E. Colla, *Conflicted Antiquities: Egyptology, Egyptomania, Egyptian Modernity*, Durham and London, 2007, p. 71.

19 J. Rodenbeck, 'Travellers from an Antique Land: Shelley's Inspiration for "Ozymandias"', in *Alif: Journal of Comparative Poetics 24, Archaeology of Literature: Tracing the Old in the New*, 2004, p. 121.

20 This version published in *The Examiner*, 11 January 1818.

21 From N. MacCaig, *Three Scottish Poets: MacCaig, Morgan, Lockhead*, Edinburgh, 1992, p. 63.

Further reading

Arnold, D., *Building in Egypt: Pharaonic Stone Masonry*, Oxford, 1991

Habachi, L., *Features of the Deification of Ramesses II*, Glückstadt, 1969

Hume, I. N., *Belzoni: The Giant Archaeologists Love to Hate*, Virginia, 2011

Jasanoff, M., *Edge of Empire: Conquest and Collecting in the East 1750–1850*, London, New York, Toronto and Sydney, 2006

Kitchen, K. A., *Ramesses Triumphant: The Life and Times of Ramesses II*, Warminster, 1982

Manley, D., & Rée, P., *Henry Salt: Artist, Traveller, Diplomat, Egyptologist*, London, 2001

Mayes, S., *The Great Belzoni: The Circus Strongman who Discovered Egypt's Treasures*, London and New York, 1959 (reprinted 2008)

Moser, S., *Wondrous Curiosities: Ancient Egypt at the British Museum*, Chicago and London, 2006

Tyldesley, J., *Ramesses: Egypt's Greatest Pharaoh*, London, 2001

Author's acknowledgements

I would like to take this opportunity to thank my colleagues in the British Museum's Department of Ancient Egypt and Sudan for their invaluable help, guidance and support with this book: especial thanks are due to Neal Spencer, Richard Parkinson (now Professor of Egyptology, University of Oxford), Anna Stevens, Patricia Usick, Marcel Marée, Tania Watkins, Derek Welsby and Marie Vandenbeusch. I would like to extend grateful thanks to Campbell Price, Joyce Tyldesley, Josefine Frank, Willemijn van Noord and Kathryn Box for their encouraging comments and suggestions during the creation of this little book, to Claire Thorne and Alice Salvador, and to Ivor Kerslake and Saul Peckham, for their beautiful illustrations and photography, to Francesca Hillier for her assistance in my navigation of the British Museum archives, to Hourig Sourouzian, The Metropolitan Museum of Art, Tomomi Fushiya and Ken Griffin for kindly allowing me access to their photographic collections and for permitting the use of their images, and to Coralie Hepburn, Emma Poulter and Carolyn Jones for their patience and energy throughout the process. Finally to my family, to Glyn Morgan, and above all to my mother Christine Garnett and my late grandparents George Henry and Joan Rowlinson for three decades of inspiration.

Picture credits

14 British Museum EA 15740.

15 British Museum EA 5601.

16 British Museum EA 55251.

17 The Metropolitan Museum of Art, Rogers Fund, 1930 (30.4.90). Image © The Metropolitan Museum of Art.

18 British Museum EA 19.

19 © Memnon/Amenhotep III Project, courtesy of Hourig Sourouzian.

20 Roemer-und-Pelizaeus-Museum Hildesheim, no. 1979. Drawing by Alice Salvador.

21 Photo © Marie Vandenbeusch.

22 From *Description de l'Égypte*, 1809–29, vol. II, pl. 25.

23 © National Portrait Gallery, London.

24 © National Portrait Gallery, London.

25 'Mode in Which the Young Memnon Head Now in the British Museum was Removed' by G. Belzoni (lithograph), *c.* 1816 / © Royal Geographical Society, London, UK / Bridgeman Images.

26 Photo © Anna Garnett.

27 British Museum Central Archives CE 115/1/199: installation of the Colossal Head of Ramesses II in the Townley Gallery, Jan 9th 1819 inscribed 'WM Alexander fac.'.

28 Anonymous watercolour: 'A Room in the Sculpture Gallery of the British Museum. February 1820. From a sketch taken on the spot in September 1819'. British Museum PD 1881.11.12.137.

29 The Egyptian Sculpture Gallery: Engraving by William Radclyffe after B. Sly. British Museum PD 1940.5.29.2 (23).

30, 31 British Museum EA 19.